Which Animals Are the Best Athletes?

Faith Hickman Brynie

I Like READING About ANIMALS!

Contents

Note to Parents and Teachers: The *I Like Reading About Animals!* series supports the National Science Education Standards for K–4 science. The Words to Know section introduces subject-specific vocabulary words for the two different reading levels presented in this book (new reader and fluent reader), including pronunciation and definitions. Early readers may need help with these new words.

Words to Know

New Readers

arctic (ARK tihk)—The large frozen area around the North Pole.

athlete (ATH leet)—Someone who is very good at sports, or is very strong or fast.

dive (DYV)—To go headfirst into water; to drop from higher in the air to lower.

Fluent Readers

balance (BAL ents)—Staying steady; not tipping over.

energy (EH nur jee)—The power animals or people use to be active.

fungus (FUN gus)—A type of plant group that includes mushrooms and mold.

predator (PREH duh tur)—An animal that hunts other animals for food.

vision (VIH zhun)—The ability to see.

Strong and Fast

Some animals seem like great **athletes**. They can run fast. They can jump high. They can **dive** deep. They are strong. They can lift heavy things.

What makes an animal an athlete?

Many things make an animal an athlete. One thing is strength. The elephant can lift more weight than any other animal can. It can pick up trees that weigh 2,000 pounds (900 kilograms).

But for its size, the rhinoceros beetle is stronger than the elephant. It can lift 850 times its own weight. The elephant lifts only about one-fourth its own weight.

Let's learn about some other ways in which animals can be athletes.

What is the fastest animal?

The cheetah does not run far. It runs fast. It is the fastest animal on land. It runs to catch other animals. It kills them for food.

How can the cheetah run so fast?

The cheetah can run as fast as a car going 70 miles (114 kilometers) an hour. But it can't go that fast for long. It can run at that speed for less than ten seconds.

The cheetah has a long, thin body. Its bones are light. The cheetah's tail helps the animal balance. The cheetah's back legs and backbone act like springs, launching the animal forward. Sharp claws dig into the ground when the cheetah runs.

Which animal wins the long-distance race?

This pronghorn antelope can run fast. It can run for a long time. It can run a long way. It can keep running for thirty minutes or more.

Which is the better runner, the cheetah or the antelope?

Over a short distance, the cheetah is faster than the antelope. But the antelope wins the long-distance race. It can run as fast as 40 miles (65 kilometers) an hour for half an hour or more.

The pronghorn antelope can get away from a predator such as a wolf or a bobcat. One reason is its excellent vision. It can see a predator from far away. Also, the antelope is very steady on grass, rocks, and hills. Before a predator can get near, the antelope has already run away.

Is this shrimp strong?

This shrimp is tiny. It does not look strong, but it is. For its size, it kicks harder than any other animal can. Its kick can break glass. ▶

What makes the kick of the mantis shrimp so powerful?

The mantis shrimp has a claw like a hammer. Its leg acts like a locked spring. The lock lets go. *Bam!* The animal's leg springs out.

The kick moves as fast as 50 miles (80 kilometers) an hour. Its force equals 100 times the animal's weight. All this power has a purpose. The mantis shrimp cracks the shells of snails and eats them.

What bird flies the farthest?

◀ This **arctic** tern flies farther than any other bird. It flies from near the North Pole to near the South Pole. Then it flies back again. It makes the trip every year.

How far does the arctic tern travel?

The arctic tern flies about 22,000 miles (35,000 kilometers) every year. Groups of terns fly nearly to the South Pole when winter comes to the north. They fly back to lands near the North Pole when winter comes to Antarctica.

The tern hardly ever rests on the waves. It does not swim. It dives into the ocean for shrimp and plant food. It keeps flying as it eats its food.

Arctic terns in Iceland

What is this gibbon doing?

This gibbon plays in the trees. It has long arms. It can ▷ swing fast and far. It can jump from branch to branch.

What makes the gibbon a champion gymnast?

Gibbons are small, so they can swing in the trees without breaking any branches. They can jump from limb to limb and keep their balance.

Gibbons have an extra joint in the wrist. It lets them turn their hands more than other animals can. They have an extra joint in their thumbs, too. It helps them hold on.

What animal is the best diver?

Which animal can dive deepest? Which can stay under water longest? Did you guess a whale? That's right. The sperm whale is the best animal diver.

How deep can sperm whales dive?

The sperm whale can dive deeper than any other animal. It can go more than a mile (1.6 kilometers) deep. It dives to the bottom to catch its favorite dinner, the giant squid.

A sperm whale can stay under water for more than two hours. Then it has to come up for air. It lives most of its life on the surface of the ocean.

Which animal jumps highest?

A kangaroo? Guess again. For its size, the flea jumps higher. Its jump may not look high to you. But it is a high jump for the tiny flea.

How high can a flea jump?

A flea can jump 10 inches (25 centimeters) into the air. That may not seem like a high jump until you think about the flea's size. That jump is 130 times the flea's height!

If you could jump that high, you could leap over a five-story building. That's higher than some skyscrapers.

What animal is as fast as a racing car?

This peregrine (per uh grin) falcon is the fastest animal in the air. When it dives, it goes as fast as a racing car. It dives fast to catch small birds.

How fast can a peregrine falcon dive?

Peregrine falcons are more than the fastest bird. They are the fastest of all animals. In a stoop, or dive, they can fly as fast as 200 miles (320 kilometers) an hour.

Peregrine falcons can twist and turn and change direction in the air. They are good hunters. They catch doves, waterbirds, pigeons, and bats for food.

What is the fastest fish?

This sailfish is the fastest fish. It lives in the ocean. It moves as fast in the water as a cheetah moves on land. ▶

How does speed help the sailfish survive?

The sailfish lives in the open ocean. It feeds on fish that swim in large groups, called schools.

When a sailfish finds a school of prey fishes, it follows slowly at first. When the time comes, it lets go with a burst of speed. It darts into the middle of the school. Then it turns and hits a fish with its long, pointed bill. It quickly gobbles up its prey.

What is this strong ant lifting?

This leaf-cutter ant cuts a piece of a leaf. The leaf is bigger than the ant. No problem! The strong ant carries the leaf to its nest.

Why do leaf-cutter ants carry such heavy loads?

Ants are champion weight lifters. They can lift fifty times their body weight. (Could you lift fifty people your size?)

The leaf-cutter ant carries all this weight so that it can grow its food. It does not eat the leaf it cuts. It keeps the leaf pieces. Soon fungus grows on the pieces. Then the ant eats the fungus.

How strong are these dogs?

These sled dogs pull a sled. They do not mind the snow and cold. They can keep going for many days without getting tired. ▶

What makes sled dogs master athletes?

At temperatures of 40 to 60°C *below* zero, sled dogs pull their heavy load. Strong winds, snowstorms, and rough ground do not stop them. In a race, sled dogs can run as far as 125 miles (200 kilometers) a day. Some dogs race for six hours or more a day. Some races last two weeks.

How far can a kangaroo jump?

Kangaroos jump. They do not jump high. They jump far. A football field is 100 yards (90 meters) long. A kangaroo can jump that far in eight jumps.

What makes the kangaroo such a good jumper?

Kangaroos cannot walk and they cannot move backward, but they are champion hoppers. They can hop as fast as 30 miles (48 kilometers) an hour. Their legs act like springs. Hopping uses less energy than walking. The faster the kangaroo goes, the less energy it needs to hop.

Kangaroos hop long distances to find food and water. They rarely need to hop away from danger because they do not have many predators.

Learn More

Books

Bailey, Jacqui. *Amazing Animal Facts*. New York: Dorling Kindersley, 2003.

Burnie, David. *Amazing Animals Q & A: Everything You Never Knew About the Animal Kingdom*. New York: DK Children, 2007.

Franco, Betsy. *Amazing Animals*. New York: Children's Press, 2002.

Rebus, Anna. *Kangaroos*. New York: Weigl, 2006.

Taylor, Barbara. *Apes and Monkeys*. Boston: Kingfisher, 2004.

Web Sites

National Geographic: Kids. http://kids.nationalgeographic.com/animals

Yahoo! Kids. *Kids Study Animals*. http://kids.yahoo.com/animals

Index

Enslow Elementary, an imprint of Enslow Publishers, Inc.

Enslow Elementary® is a registered trademark of Enslow Publishers, Inc.

Library of Congress Cataloging-in-Publication Data

Brynie, Faith Hickman, 1946–
    Which animals are the best athletes? / Faith Hickman Brynie.
      p. cm. — (I like reading about animals!)
    Includes bibliographical references and index.
    Summary: "Leveled reader that answers questions about animal athletes—including which animals are the best divers, the highest jumpers, and more—in both first grade text and third grade text"—Provided by publisher.
    ISBN 978-0-7660-3329-0
    1. Animal locomotion—Juvenile literature. I. Title.
    QP301.B8942 2010
    591.5'7—dc22
                   2008050059

ISBN-13: 978-0-7660-3751-9 (paperback)

Printed in the United States of America

112009 Lake Book Manufacturing, Inc., Melrose Park, IL

10 9 8 7 6 5 4 3 2 1

Photo Credits: Photos by naturepl.com: © Chris Gomersall, p. 12; © Dave Watts, pp. 1, 28; © Doc White, p. 26; © Doug Perrine, pp. 16, 17, 22; © Eric Baccega, pp. 27, 32; © Inaki Relanzon, p. 13; © Ingo Arndt, p. 15; © Jeff Rotman (Avi Klapfer), p. 23; © John Downer, p. 4; © Kim Taylor, pp. 19, 25; © Lucasseck/ARCO, p. 7; © Mark Payne-Gill, p. 20; © Michael Durham, p. 8; © Nature Production, p. 5; © Solvin Zankl, pp. 1, 10, 11, 24; © Wegner/ARCO, p. 14.

Photos by Shutterstock: pp. 2–3, 30–31.

Cover Photo: © Dave Watts/naturepl.com.

Series Science Consultant:

Helen Hess, PhD
Professor of Biology
College of the Atlantic
Bar Harbor, ME

Series Literacy Consultant:

Allan A. De Fina, PhD
Dean, College of Education/Professor of Literacy Education
New Jersey City University
Past President of the New Jersey Reading Association

Enslow Elementary
an imprint of

 Enslow Publishers, Inc.
40 Industrial Road
Box 398
Berkeley Heights, NJ 07922
USA

http://www.enslow.com